Psst. Hey, Kid. I'm talking to you. Yippee! You've passed the first test... you opened a book with underpants on the cover. But are you ready for the next challenge—

mastering the wedgie and every other KidSkill in this handbook of essential cool-kid knowledge? Come on, you can do it... we dare you! Okay, we double-dare you!

Bbrrooorrr...

rrr₃₃o

How to Give a Wedgie!
And Other Tricks, Tips, & Skills No Adult Will Teach You

Dave and Joe Borgenicht

Drawings by Matt Phillips

AVON BOOKS

An Imprint of HarperCollins*Publishers*

A QUIRK PACKAGING BOOK
Editor: Sharyn Rosart
Design director: Lynne Yeamans

Library of Congress Cataloging-in-publication data is available.

First Avon edition, 2005

AVON TRADEMARK REG. U.S. PAT. OFF. AND IN OTHER COUNTRIES, MARCA REGISTRADA, HECHO EN U.S.A.

1 2 3 4 5 6 7 8 9 10
❖

Visit us on the World Wide Web!
www.harperchildrens.com

When giving wedgies and popping wheelies it is important to keep safety in mind. For
example, no wheelie popping would be complete without a chic and well-coordinated
helmet. As such, the publisher and authors disclaim any liability from an injury that may
result from the use, proper or improper, of the information contained in this book. We
urge you to obey all laws and respect all rights of others.

PRACTICAL
SKILLZ

CONTENTS

KIDSKILL #1
FOLD AND PASS A NOTE

FOR SOME REASON, teachers of all kinds think that note passing during class is distracting and wrong. Don't they know that passing notes helps kids develop social and communication skills? Not to mention helping students everywhere survive science class.

THE GOAL:

To pass a note to a fellow student during class without being detected. When done well, note passing can get a lot of your questions out of the way during class so that you don't have to waste valuable time during lunch or recess getting caught up.

Passing notes without getting caught requires a good sense of timing. Generally, you can pass a note as soon as your teacher turns around. But BEWARE of the "fake out" (when your teacher turns and then turns right back around again).

THE EQUIPMENT:
- A piece of paper
- A pen (one that has a replaceable ink cartridge)
- A rubber band

Be extremely careful when passing notes. You always risk getting caught and having your note read aloud. You might want to write your note in code (see To Write in Code, p. 14).

5

THE SKILL:

There are many ways to safely pass a note without getting caught. Below you will find the most successful techniques.

"The Slingshot"

1 First, write your note.

The size of the paper depends on how far you have to slingshot your message. The farther it has to fly, the larger the paper needs to be.

2 Next, fold your note. Fold your paper in half until it is about 1" X 1" (about six times).

3 Now you should hook a rubber band over the tips of your thumb and index finger. Use your dominant hand (that is, your most coordinated, strongest hand—it's probably your right hand if you're right-handed, or your left hand if you're left-handed) to help control aim.

4 Hook your note on your rubber band. Fold your note over the rubber band so that the crease sits over both lines of the band. Hold from the top and bottom of the note.

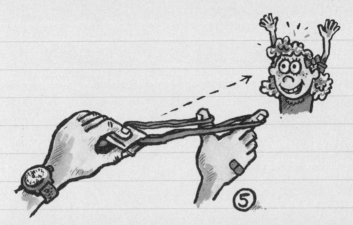

5 Pull back the note. Keeping the rubber band and the hand you're holding it with in place, pull the note back the desired distance.

6 Aim and release your note. When the teacher isn't looking, send your note flying!

Unless your aim is exceptional, be sure that your friend is waiting and ready to catch the note!

"Fake pen"

1 First, make a plan with the friend to whom you are writing: when the time is right, she asks you to lend her a pen. Then, write your note.

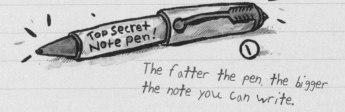

The fatter the pen, the bigger the note you can write.

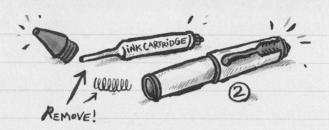

2 Next, unscrew the top and bottom halves of a pen that uses replaceable ink cartridges. Remove the ink cartridge from the pen, and set it aside.

3 Now you have your note vehicle. Just roll up the note and slip it inside the pen. Once the note is inside, you can screw the two halves of the pen back together.

4 When your friend asks you if she can borrow a pen, simply pass it to her—note enclosed.

If your friend asks the teacher for permission to borrow a pen, then she risks not getting the note pen. Just pass the pen and ask forgiveness later.

KIDSKILL #2

BOOBY-TRAP A ROOM

KIDS HAVE BEEN PROTECTING THEIR STUFF FOREVER.
This is one of the most important Kidskillz there is.

Be sure to remember which booby traps you set and where! You don't want to get booby-trapped by your own hand!

THE GOAL:

To set a series of simple traps in your room or other rooms
in the house. When correctly set up, booby traps can let
you know if someone is entering your room without your
permission, protect you and your things from the clutches
of a sibling, fend off unwanted visitors, or simply amuse and
entertain you.

Each trap is different, so the necessary equipment is listed with each setup.

"Booby-Trap a Door: Simple Seal Method"

THE EQUIPMENT:

- Clear tape, or
- A hair plucked from your head

THE SKILL:

1 First, leave the room you want to protect. Close the door
behind you all the way.

2 Next, take a small piece of clear tape and stick it across the bottom of your closed door. Be sure that the tape sticks partly to the door and partly to the frame. If the tape is broken when you return, a trespasser has tried to enter the room.

3 You can also do this with a piece of your hair. Lick both sides of the hair and stick it across the door and the frame. If your room is entered, it will detach and fall off.

"Booby-Trap a Door: Rain of Confetti Method"

THE EQUIPMENT:
- A paper bag
- Confetti

THE SKILL:

1 From the inside, carefully place a paper bag full of confetti on top of your door so that it leans against the doorframe when you pull the door not quite closed.

2 When the door opens, the intruder will be showered with confetti.

Close the door from the outside, unless you want to stay inside and watch the action when your intruder gets showered with confetti!

10

"Booby-Trap a Closet"

THE EQUIPMENT:
- Lots of toys
- Lots of clothes
- Lots of stuffed animals

THE SKILL:

1 Start by filling the bottom of your closet with soft, bulky items like clothes, sheets, or towels.

2 Next, fill the top with toys or an unassembled jigsaw puzzle. Be sure the closet is stuffed to capacity with all your gear.

The tricky part is getting the door closed! Teeter your gear toward the door, then slip out and quickly close the door.

MISC. Small Toys

SOFT BULKY STUFF

3 When the trespasser opens the door, everything will fall out onto him!

"Booby-Trap a Bed"

Booby-trapping your bed ensures that potential intruders stay out of your room while you are not there by fooling them into thinking you are actually in bed. The most effective booby trap for a bed is the "fake you." Though this trap does not physically attack your visitor, it may deter her from coming any farther into your room.

1 First, get two or three pillows.

2 Place them under the sheets as if they were a body. Now pull the covers back over the pillows, as if covering someone up.

Tape-record yourself snoring and play the tape after you leave. No one would dare enter your room with you still inside!

"Booby-Trap the Kitchen Sink"

1 First, take a rubber band and place it over the sprayer on the kitchen sink. Make sure that the rubber band presses the handle of the sprayer all the way down. You may need to wrap it around a couple of times to ensure this. (If your kitchen sink doesn't have the right kind of sprayer, you may have to improvise!)

The point of this booby trap is to get your victim wet, so before you set it up be sure to choose a time when your victim is not wearing her best clothes.

2 Next, point the sprayer directly at the front of the sink—where your victim will be standing.

3 Wait for the fun! When your victim turns on the faucet, water will come out of the sprayer and should hit her directly.

KIDSKILL #3
WRITE OR SPEAK IN CODE

EVERYONE NEEDS A CODE: speaking or writing in code is the best way to keep information secret and keep everyone else guessing what you know and they don't!

THE GOAL:
To mask your words (written or spoken) so that only you and your accomplice(s) know what is being said. With a good code you can talk about your teachers or your enemies right in front of them. Of course, if they crack your code, you are in for it! So make sure you make it tough.

THE EQUIPMENT:
- You
- A friend
- A decoder

THE SKILL:

"To Write in Code"

Start by making a codebook. After memorizing the code in your codebook, you and your allies will be able to write messages to one another that no one else can read!

The Simple Reversal, or x-l-w-v. There are 26 letters in the alphabet. The easiest (and therefore most crackable) code is one in which you simply invert the letters so that the corresponding letter at the end of the alphabet matches the one at the beginning. It looks like this:

A	B	C	D	E	F	G	H	I	J	K	L	M	N	O	P	Q	R	S	T	U	V	W	X	Y	Z
Z	Y	X	W	V	U	T	S	R	Q	P	O	N	M	L	K	J	I	H	G	F	E	D	C	B	A

In this code, A=Z, B=Y, etc. So if you were to write out the word c-o-d-e, in code, it would read x-l-w-v.

The Scramble. For a scrambled and more random code, create one that makes letters equal others in a completely random order. It might look like this:

A	J	T	N	E	I	C	M	W	Q	O	K	S
V	P	R	G	B	Y	L	F	X	Z	D	H	U

In this code, A=V, B=E etc. So if you were to write out the word d-o-o-f-u-s, it would read o-d-d-m-s-u.

This code is virtually un-crackable unless the cracker has a copy of your codebook. On the downside, though, it also takes longer for your friends to translate these types of messages.

"To Speak in Code"

First, decide which code you want to speak in.

Pig Latin. This is the most obvious code, thus the easiest for you to speak and for others to decipher. To speak in Pig Latin, take the first consonant off every word and tack it to the end of the word, followed by an "ay" sound, like in the word "way." If a word begins with a vowel, simply add the "ay" sound to the end.

"I am going to the park," in Pig Latin, is
"I-ay am-ay oing-gay o-tay e-thay ark-pay."
The downside is that unless you speak very fast,
an outsider may easily decipher this code.

Dubbi. This code is slightly more difficult for an outsider to decipher, but not impossible. To speak in Dubbi, you must add the sound "ubbi" before every vowel sound. If a vowel begins the word, then use the vowel in place of the "u" in "ubbi." At the end of the replaced "ubbi," the vowel from the word is used instead of the "i" in "ubbi."

YOU GET THE PICTURE!

"Your brother eats worms,"
in Dubbi is "Y-ubbour
br-ubbo-th-ubber eabbits
w-ubborms."

KIDSKILL #4
ACCEPT (OR DENY) BLAME

NO ONE LIKES TO GET IN TROUBLE. That's why it's important to learn the skill of accepting or denying blame.

THE GOAL:
To admit (like an honorable kid) that you did something bad. Or, if what you did is really bad, to deny that you had anything at all to do with it. (But be prepared to own up if your denial is going to get someone else in trouble.) You'll have to use your own judgment about whether you want to admit or deny that you did it (whatever it was).

It's important to think of the consequences before deciding to accept or deny blame. If the consequence is that you have to go to your room without dinner, and dinner is liver and onions, then by all means, confess!

THE EQUIPMENT:
● A poker face

The term "poker face" comes from the card game. It means that you keep a straight face, that is, show no emotion on your face, so that the other players can't tell if your cards are good or bad.

17

THE SKILL:

"Accepting Blame"

1 First, take a deep breath. (This is a good way to relax and it will prepare you to handle the scolding you are about to get.)

2 Next, look your accuser straight in the eye.

This shows that you are not afraid and are being honest!

3 Admit, sadly and humbly, that yes, you were the one who tracked mud across the floor. (Or whatever the problem might be.)

4 Next, quickly apologize. Explain that you didn't know what you were thinking. That, in fact, you weren't thinking.

5 Apologize one more time. Tell your accuser that you feel horrible about your mistake. Now for the kicker, offer to make up for it (for example, clean up the mess you made).

"Denying Blame"

1 First, take a deep breath. (This is a good way to relax and it will prepare you for the challenge ahead.)

2 Next, look your accuser straight in the eye.

Only liars don't make eye contact.

3 Deny, deny, deny that you had anything to do with what happened. Show disgust that your accuser would even think you had anything to do with it.

A few "I'm disgusted" sounds are: "Phfff. Huuu. Eegghawa."

4 Next, quickly go on the offensive. Accuse your accuser of being insulting. Try phrases like "Is that what you think of me? That I would just track mud across the carpet and not do anything about it? Thanks for the vote of confidence. I'm glad I know where I stand with you!"

5 Deny one more time. If your conscience can stand it, try to spread the suspicion to another culprit, such as your baby sister or the cat.

KIDSKILL #5
GET THE LAST WORD

THE LAST WORD: one of the most valuable commodities in the Kidskillz world today. The last word means that you are right. The last word means that you are in control. The last word means that even if you are wrong, at least you get the last word!

THE GOAL:
To be the last person to speak in an argument, thereby "winning" the argument. If you learn to do this well, then you can always be right! Everyone knows that whoever gets the last word is the one who's right.

THE EQUIPMENT:
- A sharp wit
- A person to argue with

Sometimes you have to have the last word not out loud, but to yourself. Even if this is the case, at least you know that you're right.

THE SKILL:

1 First, try to get the person you are arguing with to admit that he is wrong and you are right. If you can do this, the hard part is done; go directly to the responses in the illustration on page 21.

2 If this doesn't work, then simply agree to disagree. In other words, say that you both have different opinions but that you'll just have to disagree and go on with life.

3 Next, turn around and say under your breath, "Except my opinion is more right than yours."

4 If the person you are arguing with hears you, then you have to turn back and start all over again.

5 Once your opponent has given in, use any of the following responses until you have spoken the last word:

IF THEY SAY....
I'M SORRY...
I'M SORRY TOO....
THANK YOU...
YOU'RE WELCOME.
IT'S NOTHING.
NO IT'S NOT...
YES IT IS...

....YOU SAY
I'M SORRY TOO.
THANK YOU.
YOU'RE WELCOME.
IT'S NOTHING.
SURE IT IS.
YES IT IS.
NO IT'S NOT.

PLAY
SKILLZ

KIDSKILL #6
WIN A STARING CONTEST

THE STARING CONTEST dates back to the earliest human children. It is one of the oldest methods of proving superior stamina and retina.

THE GOAL:
To out-stare your opponent. Two contestants stare into each other's eyes without blinking, and the contestant who blinks first loses.

If you doubt that the eye can stay open that long, pay attention to movie actors in the next movie you see (one that's not a cartoon). Many actors are so focused on what they are doing that they hardly blink while delivering their lines.

THE EQUIPMENT:
- You
- An opponent
- A judge (impartial or not, depending on how you want to play the game)

THE SKILL:
To win a staring contest, you must use one of the tried-and-true tactics for a stare-down.

"The Honest Win"

1 Start with your eyes closed tightly. Keep them shut until the judge says go. The longer and tighter you keep your eyes closed, the more tears they will produce. When you open them ready to stare, they will be flush with lots of moisture.

2 Next, fix on and stare at a point NEAR your opponent's eye. If you choose one point that is close to but not directly in your opponent's eye, then you eliminate his or her ability to psych you out.

STARTING WITH EYES CLOSED TIGHTLY

①

Secretly drop some eye drops into your eyes before the contest. The wetter your eyes, the better. (This is not really cheating, just gaining a little advantage—after all, you still have to hold your opponent's stare.)

*ZITS (NEAR EYES) MAKE EXCELLENT STARING TARGETS!

THE OPPONENT

②

3 At this point you should clear your mind. Try not to think, but if you have to, you should be thinking only one thought: "Do not blink. Do NOT blink. Do not BLINK!"

It is said that yogis from far-off lands have the ability to go into a sort of staring trance. They do not think about blinking; they simply exist, and the urge to blink goes away. Feel free to try this.

4 If you feel ready to blink, squint your eyes. If you still feel like you are going to blink, furrow your brow. The squint or the furrowed brow may moisten your eyes. The sudden change in your expression might even freak out your opponent enough to blink.

5 Open your eyes extra wide. Just when you think you have to blink or your eyeballs will pop out, widen your eyes a little more. This maneuver is a leap of faith for those who have not experienced it. When you open your eyes even wider after a long period of not blinking, they will actually release extra moisture—and it might be just enough to win the contest.

"The Not-So-Honest Win"

Some of the following methods are clearly cheating. If you are not morally comfortable with cheating, if you think it is bad karma or juju, if you think that the only win is an honest win, then do not read on.

If all you care about is winning, you may continue.

1 Once you start the staring contest, fake that you are going to blink. You can use the squinting eye or furrowed brow technique to trick your opponent into thinking you were going to blink so that she blinks first.

2 Blow a puff of air into your opponent's eye, forcing a blink. A slight puff from the corner of your mouth may go unnoticed by the judge.

The defense against this move if you suspect it may be used against you is to wear glasses.

PRACTICE MAKES *perfect!*

3 Blink when you think the judge is not looking, and when your opponent accuses you of blinking, deny it. This is hard to pull off, but unless the judge sees you blink, there is no way for your opponent to prove that you blinked.

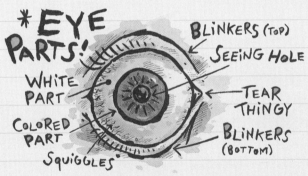

*EYE PARTS!

BLINKERS (TOP)
SEEING HOLE
WHITE PART
TEAR THINGY
COLORED PART
BLINKERS (BOTTOM)
SQUIGGLES

If you start to see stars, go ahead and close your eyes. Tears are necessary for the health of your eyes and for clear vision. Maybe you'll win next time.

Win at Thumb Wrestling

IF YOUR THUMBS ARE ABNORMALLY LARGE, perhaps due to excessive video-gaming, then thumb wrestling is for you! Your extra-big digits may intimidate opponents, giving you a psychological advantage. But be warned: large, strong thumbs do not guarantee that someone is a good thumb wrestler. An opponent with puny-looking thumbs but good technique can vanquish a large-thumbed but less experienced opponent.

THE GOAL:

To pin your opponent's thumb to his forefinger or to another part of his hand. Players grip each other's fingers, while their thumbs battle for dominance. The first one to pin and hold the other's thumb for three seconds wins.

THE EQUIPMENT:

- You
- An opponent
- Your hands

The best place to pin your opponent's thumb is over his thumb's knuckle. If you can pin the thumb-knuckle, your opponent will find it almost impossible to move his thumb out from under your hold.

THE SKILL:

Here are some tricks to get you to that win.

1 First, choose hands. Try to be the one who chooses which hand to use—then choose YOUR dominant one.

If you are not the one who gets to choose which hand to use, then do something active with your weaker hand just before your opponent chooses. This may give him the impression that your weak hand is really your strong hand, and his choice may give you the advantage!

2 Both players should make a C shape with whichever hand has been chosen for the WTF (World Thumb Wrestling Federation) Smashdown. Grip finger to finger and then pull your hands together so that you are squeezing each other's fingertips.

GRABBER!

To further intimidate your opponent, give your thumb a WTF name like "Clobberer" or "Thumb-Striker."

3 Size up your opponent's thumb with a feint, or fake attack. To do this, avoid the temptation to jump in right away with a pinning attack. Instead, dart your thumb into the ring, give your opponent's thumb a wallop, then immediately draw your thumb back. As you do so, notice where your opponent's weaknesses are. (You may have to do this a few times.) Where is he slow? Moving to the right or to the left? Moving up or moving down?

ARE YOU READY TO THUMBLE?

While wrestling, keep your fingers pressed together and your palm pulling back toward your arm to give your thumb room to maneuver.

4 Next, engage him in a tip-to-tip shove off. Put your thumb-tip to his thumb-tip and push. If your opponent begins moving his thumb from side to side, be sure to match his moves so that his thumb doesn't come out on top. Does he have as much strength as he thinks he has?

5 Move in for the pin!

EITHER ONE OF THE FOLLOWING MOVES SHOULD BRING A WIN:

"The Roundhouse"

1 Start tip-to-tip with your opponent. Give his thumb a forward shove. When he starts pushing back toward you, proceed to the next step.

2 Drop your thumb back and down to your strong side (the side where your thumb moves toward your palm). As you do, your opponent, surprised by the move, will let his thumb fall forward: this is your chance to move in for the pin.

3 Quickly slide your thumb up the back of your opponent's thumb and pin it to his hand.

"The Reversal"

1 The reversal requires that your thumb be stronger than your opponent's, so be sure you have sized her up carefully.

2 Let your opponent pin your thumb to the mat.

3 Tighten your finger grip and slide your thumb forward until your thumb-knuckle is no longer under your opponent's thumb.

4 Bend your thumb at the knuckle and push off the mat for a little clearance.

5 When you have the clearance you need, roll your thumb out from beneath your opponent's and move it to her weak side (toward the back of her hand), then quickly press your thumb across the top of her thumb-knuckle.

6 Pinch and hold for three seconds.

KIDSKILL #8
DETERMINE THE OUTCOME OF A TIE

ON OCCASION, things happen so close together that it is impossible to know who won a race, or who kicked the can, or who called the front seat first! That's why there are ways of breaking a tie, that is, "the-arrival-at-the-finish-line-at-the-same-time" kind of tie, not "the-gift-for-Father's-Day" tie.

THE GOAL:
To determine the winner of a tied contest based on the results of another contest. Assuming that the stars are aligned and fate is in play, whoever wins the tiebreaker would have won the original contest anyway.

THE EQUIPMENT:
- Your hands
- A coin
- A judge

THE SKILL:
There are several different tiebreakers available for use. Choose whichever one you think best suits your skills or luck.

HINT: If you lose the first round of the tiebreaker, insist that you play three rounds—whoever performs the best at two out of three wins. If you win the first round, congratulate your opponent and thank her for the victory.

32

"Rock-Paper-Scissors"

1 First, assume the starting position. The competitors face each other. Each holds one hand with the palm facing up and the other hand in a fist resting on top of the open palm.

2 Next, begin the count. At the same time, both competitors hit their fists on their palms. Competitors should hit their palms three times, counting out loud.

You can either count, "one, two, three" or say "rock-paper-scissors."

3 On the third count, throw your fist into one of three positions: rock, paper, or scissors.

Fist remains a fist.

Fist becomes a flat, open hand.

Fist remains a fist, with the pointer and middle fingers extended.

Slowing your personal count on the third call will give you an instant longer to see what your opponent throws. Count, "One, two (say a silent 'and'), three," and then throw. If you get caught, you can always claim you have bad rhythm.

4 Judge the winner using the following formula:
Rock beats scissors. Scissors cuts paper. Paper covers rock.

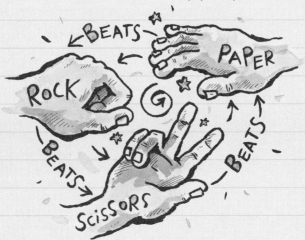

If competitors throw the same choice three times in a row, then the throw is a tie and the contest must be held again.

"Coin Toss"

1 First, find an impartial tosser.

2 Next, establish your rules. Decide whether the coin will be caught and flipped onto the back of a hand, or dropped to the ground.

Be sure to check that the coin doesn't have two heads or two tails unless, of course, the double-sided coin belongs to you!

3 Decide who gets to toss, and who gets to "call it" and when. It can be called before or during the throw.

Some say that fate shines upon those who kindly give the "call" to their opponents. Others say that when a coin is flipped, it usually lands heads up, so take the "call" if you can. Alternatively, a best-of-three Rock-Paper-Scissors may be run to determine who will "call it."

4 Tosser flips the coin. The tosser flips the coin up into the air and—based on the rules decided earlier—catches the coin or lets it fall to the ground.

5 Caller "calls it." While the coin is in the air, the caller should call either heads or tails.

6 Judge the winner. After the coin is caught or lands on the ground, the tosser should show the coin to the competitors. Whichever side the caller called determines who wins the coin toss and thus the tie.

"Pick a Number"

If all else fails, leave victory up to fate . . . or favoritism, if you know the number picker.

1 An impartial judge picks a number. This judge chooses a number between one and ten and writes it on a hidden piece of paper.

2 Decide who will pick the first number. Competitor one may offer his opponent first pick, or first pick may be determined by a coin toss or a best-of-three series of Rock-Paper-Scissors (see above).

3 The first competitor picks a number. Competitor one says the number he picked out loud to both the judge and competitor two.

4 Competitor two picks a number. Competitor two says the number he's picked out loud.

5 The judge declares the number he chose. The winner is the competitor who picked either the same number the judge picked or the number closest to it. If both competitors' picks are equally close to the judge's pick, the round must be declared a tie, and a new tie-breaking round begins.

KIDSKILL #9
POP A WHEELIE

YOUR MOM AND/OR DAD may not like this skill much because they think it's dangerous . . . but you've gotta be a kid, right? So don't do it in front of the 'rents (unless you can convince them to watch you perform it, of course) and ALWAYS wear a helmet when riding your bike (add some pads when attempting anything tricky). Never attempt a wheelie on a crowded or busy street.

If you can talk an older sibling or friend into spotting you the first few times you try this, then the parental units may feel a little better about you doing it.

THE GOAL:
To "pop" the front wheel of your bike up in the air so that you are riding and balancing on the rear wheel alone. If done correctly, this skill will allow you to travel just a little faster than your best friend, who's still riding on two wheels.

If you're riding on two wheels, then a wheelie really is the next logical step in biking skills. Think about it. You started on four—a two-wheeler with training wheels—moved up to two, and now you're on one. Have fun.

37

THE EQUIPMENT:

- Your bike
- Your balance

Since you will need every bit of your balance for this skill, DO NOT drink any caffeine or eat large amounts of sugary stuff before trying it. Though caffeine and sugar may increase your bravado, they can also impair your concentration skills and coordination, and you can't afford that. You're going to need all of your wits about you.

THE SKILL:

1 First, ready your bike. Make sure it is in good shape, with the brakes working perfectly. If you can, adjust your seat to the lowest position it can go.

There is no shame in abandoning your bike if you're going down. If you think you are going to crash, don't waste any time: hop off and away from your bike. Try to land on your feet and keep running as you land. If you cannot land on your feet, aim for a soft surface, like grass, and try to roll as you hit the ground.

2 Next, begin your ride. On a smooth, flat, and level surface, begin to ride in a straight line. If you have more than one gear on your bike, use a middle gear. If you only have one gear, pedal just fast enough to keep a straight line but slowly enough that you can hop off the bike if you have to.

3 Shift your weight. Staying firmly seated on your low seat, lean—from your waist forward—over the handlebars.

> Imagine you are ducking out of the wind so that you can go faster. You won't really be ducking the wind; you'll just look that way.

4 Pedal up. Bring one pedal up just before top dead center—about 11 o'clock. The other pedal should be down around 5 o'clock.

5 Now, crank down hard on the top pedal and shift your body weight back on your seat.

6 Pull back on the handlebars while your weight is shifted back, and watch your front wheel rise in the air. The more you lean back on your seat, the higher you'll be able to wheelie.

7 Try this move and set yourself down several times until you get the feel of being up on one wheel. Then move on to the next step.

8 Welcome to the next step. Continue to pedal. Once you have your front wheel in the air, settle into your seat. Pedal your bike keeping your arms straight and your weight centered over the seat.

Don't lean back too far. Just a little at first until you get the hang of it. Use your knees or turn your front wheel to help you balance from side to side.

9 Wheelie down. Straighten your front wheels, press down on the handlebars, and shift your weight forward to push your front wheel to the ground.

NOW SHOW YOUR FRIENDS.

Wheelie position = rear wheel down + front wheel up.

KIDSKILL #10
ACHIEVE MAXIMUM SWING HEIGHT

EVERYONE WANTS TO REACH THE TOP. Especially on the swing. It's that point where you are momentarily weightless . . . like an astronaut . . . that point where the chains on the swing loosen and then tighten again . . . that point where you're not sure if you are going to swing all the way around the top of the swing or fall back down. What a thrill!

THE GOAL:
To swing as high as you can forward and as high as you can back. To be the highest, bravest swinger in all of the playground lands.

According to the laws of physics, it is virtually impossible to go all the way over on a swing...but does a swing know the laws of physics?

THE EQUIPMENT:
- A swing
- You

You will be using your legs a lot for this skill, so you might want to do some stretches and limber up a bit before hopping onto the swing.

THE SKILL:

1 Begin to swing. Push yourself back—or get someone to push you—to start swinging.

2 Next, build your forward height. As you start to swing forward, extend your legs out in front of you. As you swing up, your body should be at a 90-degree angle to your legs.

3 Begin to build your height on the backward swing. As you start to swing back, tuck your legs underneath the swing seat. As you swing back, your body should be tucked into a "ball." Hold onto the swing chains as tightly as possible.

4 Next, increase your forward height. At the moment you start to swing forward, extend your legs out in front of you while simultaneously leaning back. Try to get your body extended out as far as you can.

Watch out for other Kids playing in your swinging perimeter—tell them to clear the area while you attempt to gain record heights.

5 Now increase your back height. At the moment you start to swing back, tuck your legs as tightly as possible while simultaneously leaning forward over your knees. Hold on!

6 You are set to achieve maximum swing height. Continue the backward and forward motions until you've reached the heights you've been dreaming of.

Maximum height is the point just before the swing goes high enough that it seems like it could go all the way up and over the top bar. You will know that you have reached maximum swing height when, at the peak of your forward swing, the chains of the swing start to fall before you do.

The chains will curl slightly and you may feel a whipping motion as your swing starts to fall, so hold on! And remember to stay in your seat!

Think about leaning back and pointing your toes to the sky.

KIDSKILL #11
MAKE YOUR BIKE SOUND LIKE A MOTORCYCLE

ONE DAY YOU'LL BE OLD ENOUGH TO DRIVE. But until then, your bike will have to do. We all know the quickest, easiest way to make your bike sound like a motorcycle is to lean forward and say, "Dvvvvvvvvvrrrrrrrr, click, dvvvvvvvrrrr, click, dvvvvvvvvvvvvvrrrrrrrrrr, click, dvvvvvvvvvvvvvrrrrr." But anyone can do that—try this instead!

THE GOAL:
To make your bike sound like a motorcycle racing along the street as you pedal it, without having to make that funny sound with your mouth. If you set everything up right, the faster you pedal, the better your bike will sound.

THE EQUIPMENT:
- A measuring tape
- Two to four playing cards
- An adjustable wrench
- A screwdriver
- A parent . . . (depending on your mechanical abilities)

With this technique you won't get the shifting sound that you get when you make the noises yourself. Instead it will sound like you are already in top gear!

THE SKILL:
1 Measure your mounting points. Note the distance from the top of your rear tire to the mounting bolt on your rear reflector. It should be around 2 to 3 inches (5–7.5 cm).

44

Basically you're looking for a place to hook a playing card that is close enough to the bike tire to be sure the card will hit it as it goes around.

2 Now measure the distance from the top of your front tire to the mounting bolt on your front reflector.

3 Punch your mounting holes. Measure from one side of the playing card lengthwise. Take the measurement from the rear tire and add half an inch (13 mm). Punch a hole—about the diameter of a pencil—in the center of the card at that mark. Mark this card "R" for rear.

Be sure to write these measurements down.

REMOVE

2-3 INCHES ①

→ MEASURE THIS

②

③

4 Do the same for the front card using the front tire measurement.

5 Next, unscrew the mounting nut. Use a wrench to remove the nut from the mounting bolts.

You can probably do this yourself if you have some mechanical skill and bike repair know-how, but it's always a good idea to ask a parent to help.

6 Slide your playing cards onto the pivot bolts. Push each card's holes over the bolt so that the long side of the card is toward the tire. That extra half-inch measurement should be enough to make the cards bend slightly across the top of the tires.

7 Replace the mounting nuts. Screw the mounting nuts back onto the pivot bolts so that they hold the cards in place over the tires.

DVRRRRRR...

8 You are ready to ride your "motorbike." Climb on and pedal. The spinning wheels should flick the card and make the motorcycle sound.

This technique works best on knobby or mountain bike tires. If you have smoother tires, look for a spot on the lower part of your front fork where you can attach a card.

Many bikes will have a bolt or knob off the frame that you can use to attach a card sideways on your bike. Fix the card on the frame so that it sticks into the spokes of the wheel. When the wheel spins, the card will flicker and make the sound of a motorcycle!

Note: if you can't figure it out, just make your own noises.

Bbrrooorrr...

Rrr 3 3 0

⑧

SpORTS
SKiLLZ

KIDSKILL #12
JUGGLE/BOUNCE JUGGLE

MANY KIDS HAVE BEEN JUGGLING since they could hold
a rattle, a stuffed animal, and a book all at the same time.
Talk about hours of fun! With a little juggling, trips to the
grocery-store produce section are better than an amusement
park. And entertaining your friends? Fuggedaboutit!

*You should be warned that juggling is
addictive. Once you've mastered the skill,
you may find yourself seeking out three
objects wherever you go. This is fine as
long as you own them. With everything,
but particularly with juggling, the rule is:
you break it, you buy it.*

THE GOAL:
To alternate throwing three objects up in the air at various
intervals over and over and over without dropping any of
them—that is, to juggle. You've seen it. You know what it is.

THE EQUIPMENT:
- Three small (about the size of an orange) beanbags
- Three tennis balls

THE SKILL:

"Juggling"

1 Start with ONE beanbag. Hold the beanbag in your left hand. Bend both of your arms at the elbows to a 90-degree angle. Turn your palms up so that they face the ceiling. Throw the bag from the left hand to the right. Catch it and throw it back again. Repeat this until you feel comfortable.

You can use a tennis ball too; it's just that beanbags don't roll away as much as tennis balls.

HiGHEST POINT

Throw your bag so that its highest point is about even with your nose.

2 Add the SECOND beanbag. With your hands and arms in the same position as before, hold one bag in your left hand and one in your right. Start with one or the other beanbag—it really doesn't matter which as long as you are comfortable—and throw it to your other hand.

3 Just before your first bag reaches its peak—at about level with your nose—throw the second bag up and to the other hand. Catch the first bag. Catch the second bag. Practice this one-two, one-two rhythm until you are comfortable.

> You may have to alter the path of the second bag slightly to the left or right so that the two bags don't collide in midair—just move your second hand a little farther away from your shoulder.

4 Add the THIRD bag. With your hands and arms in the same position, hold the first two bags in your starting hand and the third in your other hand. Throw the first bag. Just before the first bag reaches its peak, throw the second—just like before. Catch the first bag. As the second bag reaches its peak, throw the third bag.

> Practice a full series—throwing all three bags one time each—until you start to feel the rhythm.

5 Great. You're ready to juggle. If you think you've got the hang of it, have at it! Juggling above all takes practice, but once you get it you'll be able to juggle for the rest of your life. It's just like riding a bike.

> Sometimes if you look off to the horizon instead of looking for the balls, you can actually juggle better. You're able to see all three balls at the same time instead of each one individually.

"Bounce Juggling"

Bounce juggling is juggling upside down. It can be done only with items that bounce, such as tennis balls.

1 Hold three tennis balls. Just as before, hold one ball in one hand and two in your starter hand. Bend your arms (about shoulder-width apart) into a 90-degree angle. Turn your palms face down so they face the floor.

2 Bounce the FIRST ball. Just like regular juggling, you want to get one of the balls from your starter hand to your other hand—but this time by bouncing instead of tossing.

3 Bounce the SECOND ball. As soon as the first ball begins to travel up to your non-starter hand, bounce the second ball and then catch the first.

> Remember, you are controlling the balls. If you have to catch the first ball early to get your timing, just grab it out of midair. Also remember to change the path of your second ball so that the two in motion don't collide.

4 Bounce the THIRD ball. As soon as the second ball begins to travel up to your non-starter hand, bounce the third ball and catch the second.

5 Bounce the first ball again. As soon as the third ball begins to travel up, bounce the first ball again and catch the third. When you can do this over and over, you are bounce juggling.

> Also a great trick on the tennis courts!

KIDSKILL #13
PERFORM A CARTWHEEL/ ROUND OFF/SOMERSAULT

THE ABILITY TO ROLL AROUND on or above the floor has always been proof of coolness. Once you've mastered any of these skillz, like Jackie Chan or Jet Li, you too will be ready to spring into action . . . or at least have a little fun on the playground.

THE GOALS:

"Cartwheel"

To roll yourself along a line in a standing position . . . like a wheel.

"Round Off"

To start to roll yourself along a line in a standing position and then twist out of it . . . like a wheel and then a pogo stick.

"Somersault"

To roll yourself along a line in a squatted position . . . like a ball or a marble.

THE EQUIPMENT:
- You
- An open space

THE SKILL:

"The Cartwheel"

First, take the proper stance. Stand straight up in a spread-eagle formation and look straight ahead. Extend your upper arms so that they graze your ears. You should look like you are in the middle of a jumping jack. Your arms are in a V over your head, and your legs are in a V below.

You are going to cartwheel to your strong side, so be sure you know which that is (if you're right-handed, it's probably your right side but you may need to practice a few on both sides to be sure).

Next, keeping your arms up in the V position, bend your knee on the side you are moving to, lift your foot, and take a step into the cartwheel. At the same time, bend at the waist, and lean the upper half of your body downward to the ground.

Pretend that you are standing between two walls that are just wide enough for you to fit between. One wall is in front of you; one wall is in back of you. This will help you to keep your line straight.

As you put your strong hand down toward the floor, kick your opposite foot up toward your head. Imagine you are strapped to a large wheel and are being turned slowly over. Your arms and legs will move around your body with your belt buckle in the center of it all!

Look at your hands as you plant them and move through your cartwheel. This will help you keep your head up!

As your second hand reaches for—and touches—the floor, kick your other leg up. The sequence looks a little like this: hand down, foot up, second hand down, second foot up.

Let the momentum of your legs carry you over. Plant the first foot, lift the first hand, plant the second foot, and then lift the second hand. There you have it. Or as the French say, "Voilà!"

If you are afraid to go over, start with a small training cartwheel instead. Keep your feet planted. Lean slightly forward—instead of all the way to the side—and sort of jump your feet sideways over your hands. After you do this a few times, you'll be ready for the real thing!

You have to support your weight with your hands as you go over, so stay strong!

"Round Off"

A round off is similar to a cartwheel, only faster and bouncier, and lets you change direction.

To do a round off properly, you are going to need some momentum. Practice doing a few fast, bouncy cartwheels first to get the right feeling.

1 Starting with a few steps, or even a little run, repeat the steps of the cartwheel, as explained above, until you get into the handstand position. In this handstand position, instead of keeping your legs in a V as you would for a cartwheel, bring them together.

2 Now twist your whole body a quarter turn. Turn in the direction of the hand that you started with. If you started left, twist left.

3 Bend at the hips, while pushing off the floor with both hands, and bounce up into a standing position, bringing both your feet back to the ground at the same time. Bend your knees as you land.

This is similar to the landing move in the cartwheel, except both of your hands and both of your feet take off and land at the same time—instead of one at a time.

4 You should be facing the direction you came from. As you come down for the landing, squeeze your knees together. This will help you stand up faster.

"Somersault"

1 First, squat down to the floor and balance on the balls of your feet with your hands out in front of you.

Let your heels come up off the floor. If it's hard for you to find your balance on your toes, just put your knees down on the ground in front of you.

2 Place your hands on the floor on either side of your knees. Be sure that your hands are flat on the ground. Tuck your chin into your chest. Just look for your belly button—you know where that is, right?—and your chin will be in the right position.

Do you have an innie or an outie?

3 Now place your head on the floor. DO NOT PUT YOUR FOREHEAD DOWN! KEEP YOUR CHIN TUCKED INTO YOUR CHEST! The part of your head that should be touching the ground is the top, where it starts to "roll" back to your neck.

From your starting position, when you lean forward, the correct part of your head should really just settle on the ground.

4 Round your back and push forward with your toes just a bit. Your weight will already be forward, so you won't need much to just fall over yourself.

Be sure to stay tucked into a little ball. If it helps, imagine that you are a marble or basketball rolling along the ground. If that doesn't work, imagine that you are a hedgehog or potato bug.

5 As you come around (over), start to push yourself up with your hands. Set them down at your hips as you come over. Keep rolling until your feet touch the ground.

6 Now just stand up!

THROW A FASTBALL

WHEN YOU PITCH, you've got to be able to throw the heat!
Bring on the fastball. Burn past your batter. So warm up,
stretch, throw the heat, and get out there!

Throwing the heat means throwing a fastball, just in case you didn't get it.

THE GOAL:
To pitch a baseball straight across the plate at an extremely
fast pace. In other words: ball + fast = fastball.

THE EQUIPMENT:
- You
- A baseball
- A mitt
- A batter and a catcher or a strike zone against a wall

THE SKILL:

1 First, hide the ball behind your back or in your mitt. This
way your batter will not see your grip and will not know
what pitch to expect.

If there is a runner on second base, then hide the ball in your mitt instead of behind your back. The runner could see your grip and signal to the batter.

2 Next, stare down your batter. Squint your eyes as if you were squinting into the bright sun. Imagine that you are in a Western and are about to go into a duel. Or imagine that you are in a baseball game and you are about to throw a pitch.

BALL HIDDEN IN MITT

THE STARE

Use your batter stare to psych out the batter. Look past him and try not to blink. To heighten the tension, spit off to one side, but never take your eyes off the batter! (And make sure one of your friends isn't standing next to you.)

3 Now grip the baseball using one of two fastball grips:

Fingers together. With your first two fingers, grip the ball across the seams. Your fingers should be perpendicular over the point where the seams are closest together.

Fingers apart. With your first two fingers slightly apart, grip the ball across the seams. Your fingers should be perpendicular over the point where the seams are farthest apart.

4 Take your stance and wind up. Try to use the same stance and windup for every pitch you throw. That way, it will be harder for your batter to expect a certain pitch.

5 Throw your fastball. When you release your pitch, aim for the strike zone with your fingertips.

To add something extra to your fastball, release the ball from your fingertips. Be sure to follow through once you've let the ball go.

KIDSKILL #15
THROW A TOUCHDOWN PASS

THROWING A TOUCHDOWN PASS requires that you have an open team member available to catch the ball in the end zone. Once you've mastered this technique, you can tell your teammates to "just get down there." You'll get them the ball.

Throwing a touchdown pass a great distance is sometimes known as a Hail Mary pass. If you're in a game and you've got one last chance to score . . . try it. You've got nothing to lose!

THE GOAL:
To throw a football down the field—at least halfway—so that one of your players can catch it, run into the end zone, and do a little dance after she scores a touchdown.

THE EQUIPMENT:
- A football
- An open teammate
- A good arm

Beware the dance. If it's the end of the game, dance away. If you're in the middle of a game, a ref might call you for delay of game.

THE SKILL:

1 First, grip the football. Place your fingers over the laces and seams. If you have to, hold the ball back a bit—toward the narrow end—to get a better grip.

The proper grip on a football may take some time to get used to. Be patient. Practice gripping the ball around the house—just as long as you don't throw it indoors or hold it when you're at the dinner table.

2 Prepare your throw. With your weight on your back foot—which should be on the same side as your throwing arm—pull your arm back. Your elbow should be bent so that the ball is just above shoulder height.

HAIL MARY

If you're in the right position, your throwing hand and the ball should be about even with your ear.

3 Next, straighten your other arm in front of you. If you like, you can point to your target for aim, but we don't recommend doing it too early or else the other team will know where you're throwing.

4 Before you throw, adjust your shoulders. When you throw your pass, the ball will travel in an arc. Remember that the longer the pass, the bigger the arc needs to be. Dip your throwing shoulder before attempting a long pass. Keep your shoulders parallel to the ground for a shorter pass.

5 Throw your pass. Leading with your elbow, swing the ball forward. As your shoulder follows the ball, transfer your weight to your front foot. Release the ball with a flick of your wrist and fingertips.

This would be a good time to send up a prayer that your receiver catches the ball . . . thus the Hail Mary.

TOUCHDOWN!

KIDSKILL #16
SPIN A BASKETBALL ON ONE FINGER

FANCY DRIBBLES—between the legs or around the back—are great intimidating ways to walk onto a basketball court. But most everybody can do those. Not everybody can walk onto a court spinning a basketball on one finger, though! With a little practice, you too can look like a Harlem Globetrotter.

THE GOAL:
To spin a basketball on the tip of one finger. You are guaranteed to be the first one picked on any basketball team . . . though shooting is another story.

THE EQUIPMENT:
- A basketball (or two)
- Your index finger

If you get good enough at spinning one basketball, you might want to try to spin another one on your other hand. You might look a little like a circus seal, but you'll surely win friends and influence people.

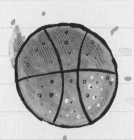

THE SKILL:

1 First, hold the ball. Hold it with your most coordinated hand (right hand if you're right-handed, left hand if you're left-handed). The ball should rest on all five of your fingertips. Extend your arm out in front of you so that your elbow is slightly bent.

2 Spin the ball up. While bending your elbow back toward you, twist your wrist in toward your pinkie. The motion of bending your elbow and twisting your wrist will spin the ball up into the air.

If you've done your job here, the ball will spin an inch or two off your fingers for a moment.

3 Catch the ball on your index finger. Think of the spin move as spinning the ball off of your other fingertips and up onto your index finger. Try to place your index finger directly under the middle of the ball.

4 Keep the ball spinning with your other hand. Hold the first two fingers of your other hand up to the spinning ball. Keep your wrist and fingers loose. With a flick of your wrist, tap your fingers on the side of the basketball in the direction that the ball is moving and keep it spinning smoothly.

The faster your basketball spins, the more easily it will land on your index finger.

Try to get a good rhythm going as you tap. It will help you keep the ball moving without knocking it off your finger.

Practice for a while at home before you take this move onto the court. There's nothing more embarrassing than trying to spin a basketball in public without success. . . . Well, maybe getting pantsed is a little more embarrassing. But getting pantsed while you're trying to spin the basketball is definitely the worst.

iMPRACTiCAL
SKiLLZ

KIDSKILL #17
WHISTLE WITH TWO FINGERS

EVERYONE KNOWS HOW IMPORTANT IT IS to be able to do things like get your best friend's attention from across the playground, call your dog, or hail a cab. And what better way to do all of those things—and so much more—than with a good, solid two-fingered whistle?

With the two-fingered whistle, practice makes perfect. Just try not to drive your parents crazy. Practice outdoors.

THE GOAL:

To make a loud whistle—the one heard at concerts, football games, and construction sites—using only two fingers and your mouth. When done correctly, the whistle should be loud enough for you to get the attention of the entire P.E. class.

THE EQUIPMENT:

- Two fingers (preferably your own!)
- Your lips

You may use someone else's fingers, but it's not recommended. You don't know where someone else's fingers have been.

A little-known fact about the so-called dog and cat calls: The dog call (wheeew wheet) is the reverse of the cat call (wheet wheeew). However, the only time it is right to use the cat call is when you're looking at your mom when she's dressed up to go out, or when you're looking at yourself in the mirror.

THE SKILL:

1 First, tighten your lips. Pull your lips in so that they cover the tips of your teeth. Tighten your lips but leave their edges exposed.

2 Next, put your fingers in place.

To whistle with your index fingers: Tuck your thumbs into the joints of your index fingers' first knuckles. Insert your index fingers into your mouth up to your thumbs. Rest your fingers on and tighten up your lower lip. Pull your thumbs away.

To whistle with your index finger and thumb: Shape your index finger and your thumb into a circle so that the tips of your finger and thumb touch. Insert this shape, tips first, into your mouth. The knuckles of both your thumb and index finger should tuck into the corners of your mouth. Tighten the corners of your mouth around your knuckles.

3 Recoil your tongue: bend it back so that the tip points up. Push your tongue forward onto your fingers. The tip of your tongue and your fingers should be at about the same level.

4 Check your setup. Exhale through your mouth. If you are using your index fingers, air should blow out over your knuckles. If you are using your thumb and index finger, air should blow down onto your palm.

If this is not happening, then adjust your fingers up or down until you feel the right path of air.

Check your tongue placement by taking your fingers out of your mouth. You should be able to produce a soft whistle by blowing some air lightly over the tip of your tongue.

5 Whistle with two fingers. Blow some air out over your tongue. The whistle is produced when the air travels over your tongue, back down to your fingers, and then up along your top lip.

IF YOU ARE NOT GETTING ANY SOUNDS, TRY THESE TRICKS:
- Tighten your lower jaw slightly.
- Close or open your mouth just a bit.
- Tighten the tip of your tongue.
- Raise or lower the tip of your tongue slightly.
- Just relax. Without the right setup, the harder you blow, the less likely you are to make a whistle.

It may take some time to find your whistle, but once you do, you will never lose it. Just like riding a bike and juggling.

KIDSKILL #18
SHORT-SHEET A BED

WE KNOW THERE'S NO BETTER WAY to say "Welcome home from your long hike, Mom and Dad," or "Sorry you're sick, little sis," than by short-sheeting their beds. Nothing says "I ♥ you" like a cramped toe after an exhausting day.

Once you know how to short-sheet a bed, you'll be set for impractical joking for the rest of your life— sleepovers, summer camps, and Grandma's house, beware!

THE GOAL:
To remake someone's bed so that when she climbs in, her feet can go only about halfway down before they hit the end of the sheet. When you short-sheet properly, you can really get someone's goat. Especially when she's exhausted.

THE EQUIPMENT:
- A victim's bed
- A flat bed sheet

To get someone's goat, milk it, and make some cheese, short-sheet with a partner. You can get the sheets that much tighter.

THE SKILL:

1 Strip the covers off of the bed. Remove all the covers—
except the fitted sheet—from the bed.

Make note of the placement and order of any stuffed animals, toys, or magazines already on the bed. You will want to put these back right where you found them so your victim will not know you were there.

P.S. The fitted sheet is the one you lie on—it has stretchy corners that hold it to the mattress.

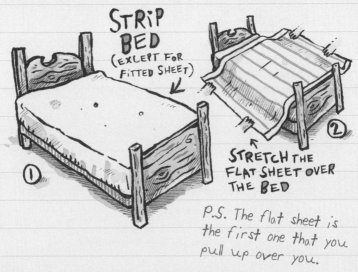

STRIP BED (EXCEPT FOR FITTED SHEET)

STRETCH THE FLAT SHEET OVER THE BED

P.S. The flat sheet is the first one that you pull up over you.

2 Stretch the flat sheet over the bed. Even out the sides
and pull the sheet cleanly up to the head of the bed.

3 Fold the foot of the flat sheet. Take the flat sheet from the foot of the bed and fold it under itself toward the head of the bed. You should fold anywhere from one to two feet (30–60 cm) in length.

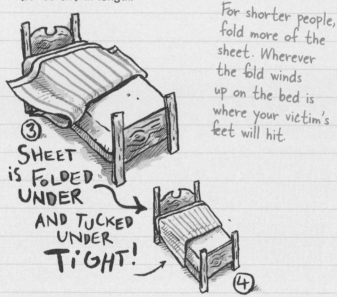

For shorter people, fold more of the sheet. Wherever the fold winds up on the bed is where your victim's feet will hit.

③ SHEET IS FOLDED UNDER AND TUCKED UNDER TIGHT!

④

4 Tighten your fold. Pull both sides of the flat sheet tight at the fold. The tighter your pull, the better the short sheet.

If you're working with a partner-in-crime, you should pull opposite sides at the same time. Keep the tension in the sheet and tuck both sides in as tightly as possible.

If you're working alone, tuck one side in and then move to the other side; pull tightly and tuck the sheet in as far as you can.

5 Re-cover the bed. Spread the covers, blankets, or comforters back on the newly made bed. Be sure to leave the top edge of the flat sheet exposed so that you can fold it back over the top of the blankets—this will ensure that your victim will slide between the fitted sheet and the flat sheet.

6 Watch the fun. When your victim climbs between the sheets expecting to stretch her feet all the way down to the edge of the bed, she will be stopped short. Humor will ensue as your victim tries to push past your tightly tucked joke. Feel free to laugh.

KIDSKILL #19
GIVE A WET WILLIE

THE WET WILLIE has been around for as long as people have had ears. Originally designed for mothers to clean out their children's ears, the wet willie quickly became one of the most annoying impractical jokes you could play on someone. Think about it: who wants someone else's finger in his ear? Especially a wet finger!

The above story is not true. But it does make sense. Just look at a kid getting his face cleaned with his mother's saliva. Is he enjoying it? No. Thus, wet willie.

THE GOAL:

To thoroughly annoy a victim by sticking one of your wet fingers into his ear and swirling it around. If done correctly, you may impair a victim's hearing for up to two minutes. This will allow you to insult him without his knowing it.

THE EQUIPMENT:

- A victim with his ears exposed
- A finger (your own)
- A liquid—either saliva or milk

Be sure that your victim cannot hear you before you insult him. There's nothing worse than an overly angry wet-willie victim.

THE SKILL:

1 Identify your target. He should be unaware of your intentions, and he should have both ears exposed.

> You can wet willie a victim who is wearing earmuffs or headphones. Just pretend that you are trying to talk to him. When he lifts up his earmuffs or headphones, sock it to him.

2 Wet your index fingers on both hands either by:

Licking both fingers and leaving a fair amount of saliva on your fingertips; or

Dipping both fingers into a glass of milk.

3 While your fingertips are still moist, sneak up on your target. Keep your fingers in front of you and always at victim-ear level. This way, if your victim turns and sees you, you may still have time to complete your task. Step very quietly and cautiously. The less your victim knows, the better the surprise.

If you cannot sneak up on your victim, approach from the front—but be stealthy. Hold your fingers down, out of eyeshot. You may even want to hide them behind your back. If your victim looks up and sees you coming, practice a little small talk: "How's the weather looking for tomorrow?" Smile and look innocent, then point over your victim's shoulder and ask, "What's that, over there?" Then proceed.

4 Insert both of your fingertips into your victim's ears and swirl them around.

5 Run. Fast.

For extra surprise and effect holler: "Wet willie...wet willie...wet willie!"

The wet willie at its most basic is the fingers-in-the-ears-and-swirling move. Here are a few tips to develop your own distinctive swirl.

Start at the outer ear and swirl, following its shape. This may tickle your victim and disrupt his attention long enough for you to complete the wet willie with a quick dip into the ear.

Swirling suction vacuum. Extra-moist fingertips are key to creating a sucking noise as you remove your finger. This tactic is tremendously irritating: master it and you will earn a reputation as a wet-willie artist of great skill.

How to Give a Wedgie

PEOPLE HAVE BEEN PERFORMING THE WEDGIE almost as long as there has been underwear. It's a great skill to learn—it can be done in almost any situation (as long as your target is wearing underwear of some sort). When it comes to getting a little harmless revenge or humiliating a sworn enemy, the wedgie is an essential skill to learn.

> Being able to properly perform a wedgie takes practice. Try a few on your younger brother or smaller neighbor before going out in the wide world of wedgies.

THE GOAL:

To pull your victim's underwear up so that it "wedges" into the crack of his or her "cheeks" and stays there for a while. If done well, it's uncomfortable but painless (unless it's a super wedgie). The victim will be embarrassed, not only because he will have fallen prey to a classic practical joke, but because his underwear will be showing.

THE EQUIPMENT:

- A victim wearing underwear
- A pair of hands (your own)

THE SKILL:

1 First, choose your victim. Your ideal victim is unsuspecting and preferably smaller than you. WARNING: Be sure your victim is wearing underwear. There's nothing worse than trying to give a wedgie on a hot day to someone who's not wearing underwear.

TRY ON LITTLE BROTHER

Good victims also include kids who don't wear belts and kids whose pants are only pulled up to their thighs.

2 Next, approach your target. Use one of the following techniques to reach proper wedgie position behind your victim:

The Distraction. Either have a friend distract your victim as you move into position behind her, or perform the distraction yourself. Drop your pencil on the floor in front of your victim and ask her to pick it up for you, or ask her to lean over and look at something on the ground ("Hey, Jenny, is this a red ant or a black ant?"), or ask her if she can touch her toes with her hands without bending her knees.

The Sneak Attack. Sneak up quietly behind your victim. Walking on your tippy-toes as close to the wall as possible will make the floor creak less.

The Fake Out. Engage your victim in a brief conversation, then pretend to leave, passing her from behind. Take a few steps away and then slowly move back into position behind her while she is not looking.

3 Once you are behind your victim, assume the position. Proper wedgie stance is behind your victim with your feet planted firmly on the ground, about shoulder distance apart. Hold your arms out in front of you—elbows bent—so that both of your hands hover over the rear side of your victim's underwear band.

The proper stance looks a lot like Frankenstein's monster—arms extended and fingers curled for attack.

I ♥ PORK

The PROPER WEDGIE STANCE

③

4 In one smooth motion, grab hold of your victim's underwear waistband and pull straight up as far as possible. Again, remember that the object of the wedgie is to wedge your victim's underwear in between the cheeks of his behind.

5 Duck and run. In most cases, the victim will spin around with fists a-flyin' to stop you from pulling up his underwear any farther. If you duck, he won't know where you are for a second, giving you the extra moment you need to get out of there, quick. Now would be a good time to run.

6 As long as you can get a few steps ahead of your victim and you've done your job right, you should be fine. A well-wedgied victim can only take a couple of steps before the discomfort of having his underpants wedged into his bottom will cause him to stop and adjust things back into a more normal position, so the farther ahead you can get now, the better off you'll be.

Watch your back for a while
after you've wedgied someone.
You may want to "go without"
for a while—at least until
bygones are bygones.

KIDSKILL #21
HANG A SPOON FROM YOUR NOSE

ONE OF THE MOST IMPRACTICAL SKILLS known to kids is hanging spoons from their faces. It's good for contests— who can hang the most spoons—but not for much else, except a couple of laughs.

There is not much danger in spoon hanging, so don't worry about being too careful. The only danger really comes when you try to hang spoons off other people's faces.

THE GOAL:
To hang a spoon from your nose using only the spoon and your nose. When done properly, spoon hanging can get the attention of all those around, and make you a little cross-eyed too.

THE EQUIPMENT:
- A spoon (or some spoons)
- Your nose

Do not assume that smaller is better in spoon hanging. It is much easier to hang a larger spoon from your nose than it is to hang a smaller one.

THE SKILL:

1 First, choose the right spoon. Novice spoon hangers should choose spoons with deep wells, such as soup or tablespoons. These spoons will be easier to hang until you get the feel of the art.

2 Next, wipe the oils off of your nose. Most spoon hanging takes place in the finer restaurants around the world, so be sure to wash your face well before you leave the house.

If you are home, wash your face with soap and water—particularly well around the proboscis.

If you are in a restaurant, casually dip one end of your napkin into your water glass and wipe down both sides of your nose.

If you are in a diner, your T-shirt will do just fine. Be sure to feel your nose for any residual oils and wipe again if necessary.

Proboscis = (fancy word for) nose.
Other words for nose = schnozz and beak.

3 Now clean your spoon. With a little water and a napkin, rinse your spoon and dry it thoroughly. Alternatively, give the well-side of your spoon a hot huff of air and then wipe with a cloth or the edge of your T-shirt.

4 Assume the spoon hanging position. Spoon hanging relies on balance. Sit up straight and look straight ahead. Imagine that your spine reaches up to and connects to the ceiling. Take a deep breath and focus your energies onto the tip of your nose. Now tilt your head up slightly so that the tip of your nose is angled upward.

Once you have hung a spoon successfully, try to stand up and walk around the room with the spoon still hanging.

5 Place the spoon on the end of your nose. Without moving your spine or head, bring the spoon up to your nose. Place it on the tip of your nose and slowly remove your hand so that the spoon hangs freely.

If you are having trouble getting the spoon to stay, flare your nostrils a bit—this will help the spoon stay in position until you can get the feel of it. Alternatively, huff on the spoon's well but don't wipe it off—the hot air may help the spoon stick to your nose.

ONCE YOU HAVE MASTERED THE SINGLE SPOON HANG, TRY TO ADD MORE SPOONS TO YOUR FACE:

- A solid smile should give you two cheek posts for two more spoons.
- Stick your jaw out a little to make a chin post. Furrow your brow for a forehead hang.
- If you have ears with "character," you may even be able to dangle two more spoons from your ears' tops.

PRETEND YOU'RE NECKING

THERE ARE TWO GREAT BENEFITS to pretending to neck. First, you don't catch any cooties. Second, the mystery of who you were making out with will have everyone wondering!

THE GOAL:

To stand with your back to a crowd and make like you are kissing someone. This skill is good for parties, entertainment, and hiding from the usher at the movie you just snuck into. When done well, pretend necking will leave your audience either disgusted or jealous.

Check out your favorite movie stars when they kiss on the big screen. Remember how they move—you'll need the guidance/tips/pointers!

THE EQUIPMENT:

• Your hands

THE SKILL:

1 First, stand with your back to the audience. If your back is directly to your audience, this will help you "hide" your invisible necking partner from view. In other words, you are standing between your invisible necking partner and the audience.

It is essential to keep your
audience between you and your
"partner." There's not much
worse than having someone walk
up to you from the front
or side while you're making a
"kissy face" to the air.

2 In the interest of making this seem real, greet your
necking partner warmly. Wave to her and take her hand
as she "approaches."

3 Next, lean in and "kiss" her. That is, as your invisible
partner gets closer, lean your head forward and pretend
to kiss her. Repeat this move two or three times to build
up to the next.

Start by kissing her the same
way you would kiss a puppy.
Kiss—kiss—kiss.

NOTE: this is not yet considered
necking—you have to build up to that!

4 Now you're ready to move into the hug. Cross your
arms in front of you and reach your hands around your
shoulders. Your left hand should be on your right shoulder
and vice versa. The audience will see your hands as
those of your necking partner. Hug yourself. Squeeze
your shoulders. Caress your back.

You HAVE TO keep your elbows tucked in front of your body. Your hands should be the only things your audience sees of your arms.

FRONT VIEW

VIEW FROM BEHIND!

BONUS! TRY SOME PRESS-ON NAILS!

5 Start the full-on "neck." As your hands move around more, "kiss" your invisible partner again. As your "kisses" become longer, move your hands up to your head and run them through your hair. Move your head from side to side like they do in the movies for those really long kisses.

YOU'RE THE HOTTEST KID AROUND!
NECKING WITH A MYSTERY KISSER!
Remember, it's essential to make sure
no one is standing in front of you
when you do this—or you'll ruin your
newly cool image.

KIDSKILL #23
PRETEND YOU'RE BEING GRABBED FROM BEHIND

IT'S NOT WHAT TIME YOU GET TO A PARTY, it's how you enter the room when you get there. A surefire way to get all the attention is to pretend that you're being grabbed from behind the door.

This skill also works great at Halloween parties, in dark movie theaters, and in the occasional classroom (especially when you're already in trouble with the teacher).

THE GOAL:
To grab yourself from behind a door so that it looks like there is someone in the next room pulling you back. When performed correctly, this skill has been known to cause fear, terror, and general anxiety in your audience members.

THE EQUIPMENT:
- A door (not see-through or glass)
- Your arms

As an advanced pretender to being grabbed from behind the door, you should keep your audience to one side of the door or the other. Do not perform this trick with direct onlookers!

89

THE SKILL:

1 First, stand in the doorway. Stand with your head and neck exposed and facing your audience in the next room. About half of your body can be exposed in the doorway, but at least one of your shoulders must be hidden behind the doorframe, out of your audience's view.

This looks as if you were just sticking your head in the door to ask a quick question.

2 At this point ask your mom if you can go out and play, ask your dad what's for dinner, or ask the other people in the room if you can come in. Whoever your audience is, the more natural you act, the more realistic the grab will be.

3 Raise your hidden arm to head level. Do not let your audience see this.

4 As your audience members answer your question, bring your hidden arm's hand behind your head to the outside of your neck and pull. Be sure to expose only your hand and part of your hidden arm. This trick works best when the hidden shoulder stays hidden.

WHEN YOU DO GRAB ACROSS YOUR NECK, IT SHOULD BE SUDDEN. COUPLE THE GRAB WITH ANY NUMBER OF THE FOLLOWING:

- *A scared face*
- *A flailing free hand*
- *A punch or kick at your "attacker"*
- *A look at your "attacker"*
- *A shriek of terror*

5 Now for the pièce de résistance: Pretend to struggle. A good fake struggle will heighten the tension and amusement.

For heightened effect, interrupt your question in step two with the grab, as if you're being caught off guard.
EXAMPLE: "Dad? Are we having macaroni and chee___?!"
Or
EXAMPLE: "Did you guys see anything strange? I thought I saw some weird guy walking arou___!"

6 Disappear behind the door with a choked holler.

"Yaaak!"
also works well.

KIDSKILL #24
SHOOT A RUBBER BAND

HOW MANY TIMES have you wanted to peg that mean kid in the rear with a sharp zing of a rubber band? How many times have you wanted the swift snap of a rubber band to "accidentally" knock the Barbie lamp your aunt got you off the mantle? And what about dropping that pesky fly right out of midair? That's why you need to know how to shoot a rubber band.

WARNING: Never shoot a rubber band at a person at close range and never, ever point a loaded rubber band at a person's eye...no matter how mean that person is.

THE GOAL:

Straight Shooter: To stretch a rubber band straight back over one hand (for aiming), using your other hand (for power and release) to shoot.

Finger Shot: To stretch a rubber band around one hand, point it like a squirt gun, and shoot—all with the same hand.

THE EQUIPMENT:
- A rubber band
- Your hand(s)

You get more accuracy with the straight shooter, but the one-handed finger shot leaves one hand free to fend off any other attacks.

THE SKILL:

"The Straight Shooter"

1 First, hook the rubber band under the fingernail of your index finger.

2 Now stretch the other end of the rubber band back toward you with your other hand.

Invert your index (shooting) finger a bit so the band doesn't catch on your knuckle.

3 Raise your arm and aim. Remember that a shot rubber band travels in an arc. So for the first few shots, aim high until you get the hang of it.

4 Release the stretched end of your rubber band with your hand. Keep your index finger as stiff as possible on release so that the rubber band can shoot off of your fingernail as smoothly as possible.

For practice, set up some empty cans in the backyard and have a quick-draw contest.

If you are shooting at a target larger than you—and one that's able to pound you—you might want to carry at least a dozen bands. Keep a few sticking out of your pocket for quick draw. And put some distance between you and your target!

"Finger Gun"

1 To shoot using the one-handed finger gun method, hook the rubber band under the fingernail of your index finger.

2 Now make your hand into the shape of a gun. With your index finger extended and pointing forward, turn your hand sideways with your thumb pointing up.

3 Load your rubber band gun. With your other hand, stretch the loose end of the rubber band around your thumb (on the back side). Bring the band down your palm. Bend your pinkie finger in toward your palm and hook the band on your pinkie.

Hook it WitH YoUR PiNKie

Keep some tension on the rubber band by stretching it slightly between your pinkie and thumb.

4 Aim. Usually for the first few shots, your trajectory will be arched and curved. Practice until you get the hang of it.

5 Fire. Roll the band off of your pinkie. Keeping your index finger and thumb straight and locked in place, pull your pinkie away from the band and watch it fly.